THE BEST ME

THE BEST ME

Venoria Todman

Mystique Journal

Miami, Florida

Copyright © 2017 by Venoria Todman

All rights reserved. No part of this publication is to be reproduced or transmitted in any form or by any means, (mechanical, electronic or any other form), without the prior permission in writing to the author/publisher.

ISBN-13: 978-0-692-98211-2

Edited by Venoria Todman

Co-Edited by Susan Cambridge, et.al

Published by Mystique Journal

Printed in the United States of America

Acknowledgement

Inspired by the need to empower others to be their best selves. *Do not let anyone tell you that you are not good enough, you cannot do something worthwhile, or you will never get anywhere. Remember you can do all things through Christ who strengthens you.*

In addition, always remember that greater is He that is in you than he that is in the world. Listen to the voice inside you and be empowered to be the best you. That is what I did, and that is why I can write to you about the best me. It is inside of you somewhere, do not be afraid to use it.

Firstly, as always, I give thanks to God *for the gift of writing and for standing by me through the tough times. Those times when I put my best foot forward, though it seemed like I was not progressing, it was* *those times that his still small voice whispered, "I will never leave you or forsake you" - Hebrews 13:5. That is all I needed to persevere and keep moving to complete the task at hand, which is to inspire people of all walks of life to be their best selves.*

*As you read **"The Best Me"**, be encouraged to take control of your life and not let anyone say to you, "You can't". I am indeed thankful for my family who has always stood by me. Gerald, Alvan, Trisha and Dion, I appreciate the love and support you have shown and continue to show me. You are my rock!*

Preface

After completing my first book in 2015, I was so excited and wanted to pen another later that year. However, things do not always happen as you plan. I am happy however, that I finally took the time to pen this new book.

*Conflicting thoughts crowded my mind as I had to decide which direction I wanted to take my audience after writing the steamy "Who Cheats More than A Politician? You Be the Judge!" I brainstormed many ideas, and this is the one I have selected for you, "**The Best Me**".*

In April 2017, I began drafting this book and realized that I had so much to say, that the thoughts kept flowing, and I could not stop writing. It was almost magical, and I felt good about it. I thank God, each day for the blessed gift of writing. It is my hope you will be inspired, as you read about the best me, to identify the best you.

I continue to be a firm believer that greatness is wrapped up in simplicity. Therefore, you may find this statement in every book that I write. Keep it simple and keep it moving. To you, my favorite audience, friends, family, coworkers, acquaintances, and all others, may you be uplifted, inspired, and motivated to be your best selves, as you read about the best me.

Foreword

You may ask why the best me and not the best you? it is simple; for me to speak about the best you, I first should speak about the best me. Just to be clear, I must first understand me before I can understand you.

I felt compelled that we can all use some uplifting, considering what is currently happening in this world. Imagine how we can turn things around for each other, if we can be our best selves. This means being more sympathetic, forgiving, loving, sharing, thoughtful, respectful, empathetic, positive, good-mannered, truthful, relatable and caring.

Imagine how this world would be, if we came together as our best selves with the above values. You may say, "that is a stretch", but if you think about it, no, not really. We were born with the capacity for the above; we just need to expand and let the best of us show, not the worst.

This book chronicles the best me as a child, sibling, student, Christian, friend, girlfriend (once upon a time), spouse, mother, college student, professor, and fashionista, the best me, today.

TABLE OF CONTENTS

Introduction……………………………..…Chapter I

The Best Me as A Child………..…….Chapter II

The Best Me as A Sibling ….….……Chapter III

The Best Me as A Student ………...Chapter IV

The Best Me as A Christian ….……Chapter V

The Best Me as A Friend …….……..Chapter VI

The Best Me as A Girlfriend
(Once Upon A time)……………..…….Chapter VII

The Best Me as A Spouse ……..…..Chapter VIII

The Best Me as A Mother……..….Chapter IX

The Best Me as A Professor……..Chapter X

The Best Me as A Fashionista ….Chapter XI

The Best Me Today……………..…….Chapter XII

Conclusion ………………………………Chapter XIII

CHAPTER I
INTRODUCTION

I will begin by introducing myself as a self-confident, motivated, tenacious, friendly and beautiful Christian woman, who knows what she wants and goes after it. Just to interject, let us not forget I am also very vocal. My hobbies include but are not limited to, reading, shopping, singing, dancing and of course, writing.

Yes, I know I can be cheesy at times. Hey, who does not like cheese? Please know my intent is not to come across narcissistic but to empower you to always be your best self, to those you encounter. Is it an easy task? No, it is not. Do I always want to show my best self? No, I do not.

Do I sometimes feel like showing my worst self? Yes, I do. Have I ever shown my worst self? Yes, I have. Does it feel good sometimes when you show your worst self? Yes, it does. Do you feel good while doing it? Sure, sometimes.

Do you feel bad and wish you never had? Yes, I am sure you do. Is it difficult to show your best self? Yes, sometimes.

The upside in showing your best self is gratifying. Whatever the situation was, you made it better. Good always trumps hate. Therefore, let us explore the best me path and see what happens.

CHAPTER II
AS A CHILD

Being the middle child of eight, I believe I matured faster than most girls my age. I was my dad's favorite, and I felt it, just as my siblings voiced it. Here we go again, I am repeating it.

Very petite with long, thick, beautiful hair, I often felt I was the envy of my siblings and some of my peers at school, for I was very fashionable.

For those of you who do not know, Venoria was and is the way to spell fashion, even from a child. Every outfit had to match, and every strand of hair had to be in place. (We will discuss the fashionista side in a later chapter).

The best me as a child was being loveable, cute as pie and jovial. In addition, I cannot forget the brains that went very well with the beauty.

Yes, you are probably saying I am and feeling narcissistic. No need to feel that way, as I am just telling you the facts about the best me. I was also very caring and considerate as a child, wanting to share my toys and whatever little I had, with others.

Think about having five sisters and two brothers, with only dad working and mom at home. Everything had to be shared, even a can of soda, which was a privilege if you had one to share. How was I being my best self?

I tried not to give my mother much grief as she had so many of us to "deal" with, especially girls. Being forthright with my mom and everyone else, even to this day, is the only way I know how. Therefore, what you see is what you get. I cannot pretend, and if asked a question, I provide a straight answer.

If I do not know something, I admit I do not know the answer. Think about it. If you say you know when you do not, you will never know, will you? Therefore, come clean; admit you do not know and learn something. That is one of the best ways to be your best self.

I enjoyed talking to my mom. She was the queen of the castle and she made me laugh so much. Her laughter was infectious, and I loved it. I listened to her when she spoke to me and tried to adhere to every word.

My goal was to avoid getting in trouble, and rather make my mom proud, while demonstrating much respect and adoration. I am proud to say my mom is unique.

She is very respectable and usually keeps to herself. Not causing trouble for others, that was and is her best self. I can proudly say she has passed that down to her children.

Another best me as a child, was giving back to my mom what she had given to us, so much laughter. If my mom seemed a little down, I did my best to cheer her up. In addition, I often tried to get her to be more vocal.

Mom was very introverted, and I am the opposite, as I am an extrovert. I tried to extract the information from her, because I could tell when she was not providing the entire "story".

It was often, because she thought we were too young to understand. If I was breathing, I wanted to know it all. Once I am informed, I know how to proceed. Therefore, give me the information and let me decide what to do with it. Oh boy, always a fiery one.

The best me took pleasure in styling my mom's hair. It was so beautiful, and I loved it. (You cannot be into fashion and not love hair, the entire "make-up" of one self)!

Yes, that was me. The controller of all things and everyone. That is me being the best me; bringing out the best in others, even as a child. If I could at least get you to laugh with me, I was, and I am "good".

My mom was the mom of all mothers. I love her to the heavens and back. She selflessly gave of herself and did not look for anything in return. I admire everything about her and am proud to be her daughter.

As a child I welcomed the times my mom would sit with us and share so many stories and jokes. At times, we all gathered in her room, and on occasion, did not leave until morning.

Those were precious moments we shared; enjoying her smiles and laughter as she told us many funny tales. This also brought us closer together as siblings.

Mom was and is seldom sad, and I believe that is why to this day, I prefer laughter over sadness. Even in my darkest hour, no one will know it is not my best day, as I try to maintain a positive outlook, irrespective of how my day is going.

As I was growing up, I saw the struggles my parents endured. Therefore, I looked forward to when I could contribute and give back to them.

When I began working, shortly after completing high school, I was determined to assist financially. Being her daughter, I also enjoyed having nice things, including beautiful furniture.

Therefore, after receiving my first paycheck, I thought of what I could give back and bought her a beautiful antique furniture set, which is still in her living room.

It took my entire paycheck, but it is something that I wanted to do for my parents who had done so much for me. This was me being the best me as a child.

My mom is very shy but at the same time makes everyone feel welcome. As a mother, she made sure we always had clothes on our backs and food on the table.

In addition, she taught us the importance of being appreciative and sharing. She also taught us not to be jealous or envious of others, especially not knowing how they had acquired the things they had.

With her teachings, we were grateful for what we had and tried not to complain. This is part of the best me I inherited from my mom and have instilled in my children.

My mom has developed dementia, and this has provided all of us with the opportunity to be our best selves to her. We strive to do this each day in trying to give back everything and more, that she has done for us through the years. We are determined to do this in every way possible, and will not have it any other way.

It is sad to see our mom this way; a woman who was so full of life and laughter is now basically immobile and must depend on others for help in every aspect of life.

Being your best self to your mom who took care of you from birth to an adult is not and should not be a question. You should be happy taking care of your mom who now needs you more than ever.

I am reminded of the songwriter that wrote, "for the nine months I carried you no charge, for the nights I've sat up with you no charge…. when you add it all up, the real cost of my love is no charge".

That is what mothers do, and we, who are now mothers, understand the sacrifices made to bring us to where we are today.

There should be no debate to be your best self to a mom who did it all for you. The Bible tells us, "honor our parents that our days may be long". However you choose to honor them, you need to.

Shout out to my sister who, in the time of need, decided to honor our mom with a living facility to avoid going to a nursing home. Nursing homes are not inherently bad, but knowing our mom, her preference would be family instead of strangers. Thank you, Sis, for all that you continue to do.

To my other siblings in the Virgin Islands, who are continuously doing what you can for our mom, shout out to you also. It is hard with your immediate families, but it is great when families can stick together and do what needs to be done for their loved ones.

When I visit my mom, I sometimes must find that special internal place to avoid falling apart. Imagine not knowing anyone, especially your children, grandchildren, or great grandchildren.

Imagine your mom not being able to laugh or converse with you. Imagine her not being able to understand or know how much you love her. One never knows, so you need to still say "I love you" and hope that she hears and understands.

It is very painful; therefore, use the opportunity that you now have, as it is the only one you are sure of. Be your best self always, especially to those you love, for tomorrow is not promised to anyone.

We tend to forget dads, but my dad was a fun guy and loved his family dearly, right down to his last breath. He was all about family. He would have done anything and everything to protect us.

I am grateful for the many years of fun, love, and laughter with both my parents.

They were there for us in different ways, and we love them very much.

Dad is looking down on us, and we know we will be reunited with him. We are grateful however that we still have Mom with us, and we will continue to cherish each moment.

Prior to my mom's dementia, she was so much fun, and even now that she is in her own space, I am glad that I still have those moments when she chuckles. I can truly say that the best me in me is credited to my mom and dad.

CHAPTER III
AS A SIBLING

There is much love for my brothers and sisters. Growing up with so many of us, some may say, we did not really need friends, but we did. My sisters and brothers often looked to me to say what they were afraid to say and to date, most of them still do.

The words shy and timid were not in my vocabulary and they knew it. As the fourth child, and a girl, I felt so blessed to have three older sisters that had my back and two younger brothers and two sisters, that I felt I controlled.

Throughout the years, as we grew up, got married and had our own families, it was and is sometimes difficult to stay in touch with everyone.

With all families, though, you find that one or two sibling(s) towards whom you gravitate. This usually occurs due to constant communication and easy access.

As a result, those are the ones you continuously listen to, cry, and laugh with. You open your hearts to them and call them "friends".

I have that experience with most if not all my siblings, but especially with two sisters. We have become very close friends. Yes, we talk about each other, and as always, they look to me to be straight forward. In addition, we share everything, and I do mean everything.

One of the two sisters, with her sharing so much, gives me the opportunity to be my best self to her. She looks to me to tell her what needs to be said and not what she wants to hear.

I often remind her that, depending on what she is asking, the answer can be brutal. I can only be the best me by being truthful. If you are seeking advice would you want to be told the truth or receive false information?

What good would there be in responding if you cannot provide the truth? Furthermore, why provide false responses or hold back? I am a firm believer in receiving accurate and complete information, so I can make an informed decision.

That is what I expect for me, and that is what I provide to those who seek guidance. My siblings know that I do not hold back, and they love it. I call a spade a spade, and my words may seem a little harsh, but they know I have their best interests at heart.

Both sisters are often advised to not seek my guidance if they do not want to know the truth. The best me does not believe in pacifying a situation. We find there are times when you are asked to be honest and when you provide the truth, those requesting your advice cannot handle it. Therefore, be careful what you are asking if you do not want to know the answer.

With my sisters, this is not the case. They may seem hesitant but are usually receptive to the advice given. I believe the truth always prevails, and should be offered to those who seek it, the truth and nothing but the truth.

You can never be the best you if you tell people what they want to hear, rather than what is. It is not beneficial to anyone and it defeats the purpose of striving to be your best self.

This sister believes she is the sister of sisters. She is happily retired and indulges in the finer things of life. In addition, she has finally or almost grown up. There are, however, some aspects of her life to which I am still providing coaching.

Her fun-loving side is contagious, especially when it comes to dancing. In her mind she is the number one Caribbean dancer. Nevertheless, every song she dances to, the dance moves remain the same.

From a business aspect, unlike me, she is not a risk taker, and because she has been a teacher by profession, she sometimes reverts to classroom mode and acts like we are her first graders. I love you Sis.

My other sister, who I am very close to, is a special character. She is all attitude. It does not matter what the circumstances are or the topic of discussion; she comes out swinging and asks questions later.

I believe she occasionally converses in her head and thinks the other person is hearing her. She asks the question, responds to her question, waits for you to agree, and simultaneously makes it impossible for you to answer. When you try responding, you are again interrupted.

I have had several opportunities to coach her in her approach. That is me trying to be the best me to her in her time of need. I cannot let her believe it is ok, when it is not.

Recently, I told her to please check her tone when communicating, or she is going to push people away. It is difficult to communicate effectively, if emotions are in play. Therefore, we need to look at what we are trying to accomplish and keep things in perspective.

Additionally, I have had to cautiously advise her that listening is part of communicating; allowing each person a chance to speak and reiterating to respectfully listen.

You make your statement or ask your question and then let the other person respond. Above all, never lose sight that communication takes place with at least two persons, unless you are communicating with yourself.

Therefore, I must be my best self to my sister and make her aware that she needs to have a much calmer disposition, if she wants things done. This is especially important if she is seeking help on the job, at home, or even at play.

One of the ways I am also my best self to her is letting her know "I am hanging up the telephone until you come to your senses". That is me being the best me to her, so we can remain friends and I can maintain my sanity.

I continuously advise her to remain calm and not let other people's opinions get the best of her. Additionally, she is reminded that everything does not need to be dramatic. Some things are and can be resolved in silence.

With these two sisters, I share the best me with them, and they share their best selves with me. And like sisters, there are many fun secrets that we have for each other.

Yes, there are many. What are sisters for? Everyone has secrets but despite those secrets, be good to each other by being the best you. In addition, remember, you are not to share secrets that are meant for your ears only. That is part of you being the best you.

It is refreshing when you have a close relationship with family members and can avoid having to continuously reach out to others. When you can confide in those closest to you, you can truly say that you are blessed.

CHAPTER IV
AS A STUDENT

As a student, my studies were continually important to me. I thrived on being the best student to make not only my parents and teachers proud, but to make me proud.

I invested much time and energy in my courses, and throughout grade school, always came in first, second, or third. Additionally, I participated in spelling bees and Christian Education competitions, representing my school well and succeeding.

In high school, my goals were pretty much the same, and I was placed in the Arts & Science field. Since I was also interested in business, I took the initiative and enrolled in business courses.

My teachers and I were in sync and eventually became friends. How often do you gain friendship with your teachers? They saw the potential in me, and I was respectful of them.

Furthermore, they encouraged me to be the best in whatever I was doing and instilled in me that there is nothing I cannot achieve, if I put my mind to it. This motivated me to be the best me in attaining my education.

As a college undergraduate, I was excited in my pursuit for an Associate of Arts degree in Executive Administration. However, it was a tough time as my first born was only three months old.

College was an exciting time, as I was now in the company of professors and older students. My academic future was uncertain, as success is never guaranteed.

One advantage of college life is that it challenges you to maintain and/or become your best independent self. Nonetheless, not everyone is inclined or motivated to succeed.

My goal was to be the best me in every aspect of life on and off campus, and exceed my professors' expectations. I am proud to say that is exactly what I did. It is true that there is no limit to what you can accomplish with discipline and determination.

I studied for endless hours, worked full time, and balanced my home life, work life, and college. It is called multi-tasking, which also brings out the best in me. How about what brings out the best in you?

After much perseverance, and commitment, I graduated with an Associates of Arts degree. I knew this was a step in the right direction for greater things.

Shortly thereafter, I was given the opportunity to work in the Financial Aid Office at the college I attended. Working with the administrative staff, students, and faculty, inspired me to attain higher goals.

I was motivated to pursue a higher purpose in life as it relates to my education and career aspirations. Additionally, I felt there was no limit to be the best me in all facets of life. Therefore, I sought out challenges and welcomed new opportunities to reflect me being the best me.

Working at the University provided me the opportunity to be a role model to the students, while providing them with guidance in their academic and financial goals.

As the financial aid officer assistant, I was tasked with advising the students regarding the pros and cons of obtaining student loans. Applying for a loan is easy; having to repay it can be very stressful.

The best me encouraged students to only apply for the necessary amount and not the amount that was available. This is a challenge for most families as their teenagers embark on the college journey.

Having the opportunity to work with the financial aid officer equipped me to provide the guidance to assist said students with their decision making, relative to withdrawal of student loans.

Additionally, while working in this role, the best me encouraged the parents to support their children in their educational goals and financial challenges. This will assist in prohibiting them from having to work to mainly pay off student loans.

I know some of you are wondering if I applied those same principles while in college. I can unequivocally say that the best me adhered to the same ideologies presented to the students. To do otherwise will not be true to my brand.

Moving forward, I returned to college and attended Trinity International University, where I obtained a Bachelor's degree in Human Resources Management. This was followed by an Executive Masters of Business Administration (EMBA) degree from the University of Miami.

As a student, my peers were enthused with my jovial spirit and desire to succeed. I often advised them that there is nothing you cannot do if you are determined and willing to apply the discipline to accomplish your goals.

What is the best you that you have discovered as a college student? Are you willing to help your fellow students who may be struggling in their studies, or do you not care? What about the students that may not seem to fit in?

Do you treat those students like the other students, as though they are better because they may dress in designer clothes or be of a certain social class? Are you ashamed to sit with that student who does not look or sound like you?

The best me has been in the company of students who felt alone and isolated and has befriended such students. Wouldn't you want someone to reach out to you if you were in that lonely space?

In situations that you are uncertain of, always ask "what would Jesus do?" Then you will know what to do. It may not be popular or cool, but it is the right thing. When you recognize your best self, and utilize those strengths to help others, that is a good thing.

The best me identifies the need to be a friend to the friendless, a shoulder to cry on, helper with studies, and someone to speak or listen to. Take a moment and ask yourself, who is the best you that is ready to "take off" and soar? I am being the best me. Are you being the best you?

CHAPTER V
AS A CHRISTIAN

You are never too young or old to accept Christ, and I can proudly say I became a Christian at the age of nine. There have been many storms in my life, but I will not exchange this life for anything. My walk with Christ is not a bed of roses but it is me being the best me.

I am aware some of you may be thinking a nine-year old is too young to understand the need for Christ, but you are wrong. Think about the things some nine-year old children are involved with today, some bad and some good.

For the negatives; having babies, stealing, sex (some of which are with multiple partners), staying out of school, drugs, disrespecting parents and other authoritative figures. It is not a pretty list and is shocking for some, but these are some of the activities in which many of our youth get involved.

Now, let us look at the positive; excelling in school, founding various products, becoming top musicians, getting signed to major labels, excelling in sports, writing, and much more.

Bottom line, at the age of nine you are old enough and can decide if you want to go on a positive or negative path. With the correct guidance, you do know right from wrong at an early age. Therefore, you can demonstrate what you have been taught.

In addition, there are those that can make serious decisions from an earlier age. Consequently, at the age of nine, you can decide to accept Christ into your life and follow the path he has for you if you so desire.

As a Christian, the best me reflects Christ in me, desires to continuously do good, and encourages others to do the same. I am invigorated to be a witness and encourage others to come to know Christ. The best me is "not ashamed of the Gospel of Jesus Christ, for it is the power of God unto salvation" -Romans 1:16.

It is the best me in me that exemplifies my Christian faith. I know who I am and Whose I am, and nothing or no one shall separate me from the love of Christ and walking with Him.

The best me knows that I can do anything and all things through Christ who strengthens me. I am also aware that "no weapon formed against me shall prosper" and "I am more than a conqueror" - Isaiah 54:17, Romans 8:37.

In Christ, there is no limit to what he can do for us. He loves us unconditionally and laid down his life for us so that we can be free.

Readers, the best me is aware that when you take a stand for Christ you may lose friends, but the best me also knows that you lose them because they were never your friends and are not of

Christ. Take comfort in knowing it is ok, for as quickly as you lose you also gain.

Those who are of the household of faith and walk in faith as you walk are waiting to welcome you. In addition, those who are looking forward to hearing Him say "well done good and faithful servant", will embrace you.

Just to reiterate, there is much in common with those who are of the same faith. You will discover that you enjoy spending time in God's word and sharing His word with others.

When you have witnessed to someone and that person accepts Christ, it gives you joy knowing that you were instrumental in that person's decision to live for Christ.

It is the best me that motivates me to pen this book, so that someone will be blessed and be bold in their Christian walk.

My desire is that all will come to know Him and be unafraid to stand for righteousness and goodness. I am reminded of the words in a song that state "after you have done all that you can, stand".

As a Christian the best me tries to be slow to judge, tame my tongue against the temptation to gossip, and focus on other areas that will be uplifting and fulfilling.

What does gossiping really do to a person? It takes too much time and energy. You can utilize that energy into something positive and be more productive.

If we take the time to brainstorm, we will realize there is so much that we, as Christians, can devote our time doing. Furthermore, we need to explore the many ways to enrich our lives while winning souls for Christ.

There are many that are yearning for the word of God and to know that they are loved. As Christians, we have that responsibility to spread God's word.

In doing so, we will demonstrate our best selves, representing the best of the best, our Lord and Savior, Jesus Christ. Imagine how this world would be if we as Christians practice what we preach.

The best me looks for the good in everyone and is willing to give each person the benefit of the doubt. Simultaneously, the best me recognizes when someone is not being honest, brings it to the forefront, and is unapologetic.

I believe in keeping it real. The way I try to do this is by being respectful, not portraying myself as better than anyone and correcting with a humble spirit.

You may say something a million ways, and one of those ways will stand out and can have a negative or positive impact.

Most times, it is not what is said but the tone that is used. Therefore, let us be mindful in our communication that we do not offend those who seek wisdom and understanding.

The Bible says, "if you humble yourself you will be exalted and if you exalt yourself, you will be abased" – Luke 14:11. Do not make anyone feel less than they are while looking to you to for spiritual advise.

I know it is easier said than done, but that is why we continue to look to Christ for his guidance and "consider ourselves lest we are also tempted".

The word of God continues that we are to "gently restore the fallen" - Galatians 6:1. When was the last time you uplifted someone?

Let us always be mindful that we are all sinners, except for the grace of God. Furthermore, let us strive to demonstrate humility in all that we do and say, so that someone will see Christ in us and come to know him.

Today, it is difficult to live a Christian lifestyle where everyone is trying to fit in. However, the best me realizes that, as a Christian, I do not need to fit in. I need to stand out. Therefore, to the 21st century Christians, you are encouraged to do the same.

Remember, the Bible states, "come out from among them and be ye separate" - 2 Corinthians 6:17. Do not try to buy-in to the things of the world, but let us have the world mirror us.

As a Christian, the best me needs to reflect something different, that others may seek to know the God of my salvation. It starts from the home. Be a witness to your children, spouses, parents, and siblings.

You would want to set your house in order, that you may be a light in the world, so others may see Christ in you and desire to come to know him. It is not easy to live a Christian life, but he promises he will never leave us or forsake us. For me, that is all the assurance I need.

As a young Christian girl, I was delighted to know the Bible. Therefore, I read it several times from cover to cover. Each time I read a verse, I gained a better understanding and new meaning.

The more I read, the more I desire to continue. It is the only Book I never get tired from reading, and it is the only book you can read repeatedly and gain something new each time. That is the working and manifestation of the "Holy Spirit".

Living as a young Christian in my hometown, I was very involved in the church, and at the age of approximately fourteen, I was a part of a singing group called "The Harmony Four".

We were committed young ladies, and enjoyed what we were doing for the Kingdom of God. Our voices blended well together, and we metaphorically sang the roof off whenever and wherever we sang. It was a magical time.

After marrying the love of my life and moving to the United States Virgin Islands, both my husband and I were actively involved in the church we attended.

We participated in various ministries, however we were mostly drawn towards the youth and desired to work with them, as we were also in that age group. In addition, we are firm believers in prayer, therefore we prayed continuously and After much prayer, we were appointed the youth leaders.

It was an honor and we were blessed to provide leadership and counseling where needed. As time went by, the youth group continued to grow, and a singing group was formed.

This group was comprised of four young ladies, including myself and the youth band. We were called "The Angelic Voices". You guessed correctly. Our voices were like angels. We sang throughout the Caribbean and the United States Virgin Islands, holding concerts and being the guests at special community events.

I enjoyed singing, especially having suffered at a young age from laryngitis. I did ask God to heal me and He did. Consequently, when I resumed singing, I gave honor and glory to Him and worshipped Him in song with the voice He had given me.

Do you believe in miracles? I sure do. Since that time, many decades ago, I can truly say that I was healed and have not experienced any problems with my voice.

There is nothing too hard for the Lord to do, and because of God's healing, I could be the best me in every area of my life. I do not need special approval from anyone as God has already approved when he created me in his own image.

I am reminded of a time in the Virgin Islands when one of the local churches invited our pastor to preach at a special church service held within the community. Unfortunately, he did not know they also expected the church choir to sing at the event.

Henceforth, when they called on our church to sing, few choir members were in attendance of the service. This was very disappointing, as we tried to support the pastor when called upon to attend community churches' activities.

Nonetheless, our pastor took to the stage and to our surprise announced we did not have the choir, but we had the church's soloist. The few of us who were present wondered who the soloist was as such a person did not exist.

Well, surprisingly, the soloist happened to be me, yes, little me, Venoria Todman. I initially panicked, but as a child of God, you should always have a song in your heart.

Therefore, the best me went on stage, took the microphone and sang a song, "Unfinished Task". There were many cheers, tears, praises to God, and a standing ovation. It was truly an honor, and I was humbled.

From that day forth, until I relocated to Miami, I was called upon every Sunday in my church to sing as the church's soloist. As the late Andre Crouch sang, "How can I say thanks for the things he has done for me? Things so underserved, yet you gave to prove your love for me"; I was and am truly blessed.

When we relocated to Miami a few years later, it took us a few weeks to find a

Spirit-filled Church, but we eventually did and currently still attend. Blessings are poured out each Sunday as the man of God delivers God's word.

To continue singing, I joined the church choir. Nevertheless, as my family grew, I could not commit to rehearsal. Therefore, I exempted myself and discovered other ways to represent Christ and do his work.

I have realized that being the best me as a Christian also involves having patience, being kind, selfless, and so much more. It includes displaying the fruits of the Spirit which are "love, joy, peace, forbearance, kindness, goodness, faithfulness, gentleness, and self- control" - Galatians 5:22-23.

In the business industry I am in, I am faced with these challenges daily. However, I find working with diverse customers provide me with the opportunity to practice all the above.

That is being the best me at work with clients, management, co-workers, and others.

What about you? Do you take the opportunity to demonstrate your best self or do you try to blend with the crowd to feel better about yourself? Do you need to be validated or are you self-confident?

Are you easily persuaded to be like others instead of being like Christ? God's word says to "let your light so shine before men that they may see your good works and glorify your Father who is in heaven" – Matthew 5:16.

We need to take each moment given to us and be a light in this sinful world. Each day, there is something new we can do for the Kingdom. Something that will be pleasing to God. How do we do this?

This can be done by being our best selves. Simply smiling with those we meet, praying for the sick, providing shelter for the homeless, feeding the hungry and so much more.

These are all selfless acts. Why pray for someone who is hungry, and you have the means to make a difference in that person's life? Let us not be ashamed to stand up for Christ, for if we are, he will deny us when we stand before him.

Matthew 10:32-33 states "whoever acknowledges me before others, I will also acknowledge before my Father who is in heaven. But whoever disowns me before others, I will disown before my father in heaven".

No one said being your best self will be easy, but you have the power to be exactly who you want to be. There is no reason to try to be like someone else. You are unique and wonderfully made.

Remember you were created in God's image so love yourself. Do not let anyone tell you anything different. Be happy with who you are. I choose to be the best me. How about you?

CHAPTER VI
AS A FRIEND

What is a friend? Some people are at times confused between friends and acquaintances. The true definition of a friend from my standpoint is someone who loves you and is always there for you.

There are many definitions online and in the dictionary, such as "a friend is someone whom one knows and has a bond of mutual affection".

You do not have to speak to your friends each day, but you know they are there for you when you need them. You have their backs, and they have yours.

I do not have many friends, and that is by choice. The best me prefers one good friend vs ten phony ones. Yes, I said what everyone is afraid of saying. I am always about quality vs quantity, especially when it comes to allowing people in my space.

Think about it: Why should you be subjected to hundreds of so-called "friends" who absolutely do not care about you. They are just pretenders, and the minute you turn your back, they gossip about you.

No one needs that in their life. I know some of you may think you need them to feel like you are part of a special group; that is not true, so do not engage in recruitment. Friendship comes naturally; it is not forced, and you should easily recognize it.

My true friends, undoubtedly, represent the make-up of less than the fingers on my hands. I enjoy being with them, laughing, speaking, reminiscing and shopping. Anything and everything you can think of, I enjoy with those who are allowed in my space.

How about friends of the opposite sex? Do you have any? My guy friends are approximately two or three and I limit the time or topics of discussion as it can be complicated, especially if you are married.

You should be respectful of each other and not cross boundaries. This, however could be a separate book as we will be treading into a complex dynamic with friends of the opposite sex.

With my girlfriends, there are no limits to what we can discuss or the amount of time we can spend together. The best me is concerned for them, and I desire that they be happy.

I do not like to see my friends sad or know they are hurting. It is important that I listen and understand their struggles and concerns. It is those times you are reminded of the true meaning of friendship.

The best me tries to be there when they need me. I see them through the good and bad times, for that's what friends are for. If you only provide support through the good times but withdraw yourself during the bad times, that is not being a true friend.

Additionally, the best me does not take advantage of their vulnerability. I do not kick them when they are down and laugh at their mistakes. The best me recognizes their faults but loves them anyway.

No one is perfect, and as a friend you should not hold your friends to a higher standard than yourself. As friends you should be in sync with each other and lift each other up, not pull each other down.

Friends are very rare, and when you find one, you should cherish that friendship. The best me tries to avoid gossiping about my friends as I treat them the way I expect to be treated.

As a friend, you should protect your companion, for that is what friends do. Avoid engaging negatively in conversations with acquaintances who may be jealous of your relationship.

The best me believes that if you do not have anything good to say about someone, be wise and refrain from speaking. Remember, silence is golden.

Do not be afraid to stand up for your friends. Be bold and do not let others smear their reputation because of pettiness. Be your best self to them even when they are unaware that they are under attack. This demonstrates your commitment to the friendship.

If you find yourself not willing to stand up for your friends, chances are you are not a friend. Real friends last a lifetime and are not to be taken for granted at any time. Acquaintances come and go, therefore, be sure to identify your true friends and avoid confusing acquaintances for true friends.

How are you as a friend? Are you that self-centered friend who makes it all about you without lending a listening ear? Do you not show concern or respect, and do not take time for your friends while expecting them to make time for you?

Look internally, and if you are that person, you need to examine your relationship and see if you are truly deserving of that person's friendship.

Friendship takes time to formulate, and when you have built that trust you protect it. Will you be the best you to those you call friends, as they are to you? When they are not feeling the friendship, will you reassure them that you still care?

If I have wronged a friend, the best me will also ask for forgiveness and make it right. If you ignore the situation, chances are you may lose the friendship.

It is better to mend fences and be humble than to stay in your own world, whether you are right or wrong. If that friendship is true, you will do what needs to be done for restoration.

Many use the word "friend" lightly. Please know there are friends, and there are "friends". One of my true friends and I sometimes do not speak for several months, but when we do, it is like we were speaking every day without losing a moment.

True friends can easily reconnect without any negative residual feelings due to lack of constant communication. In addition, true friends are difficult to find. Therefore, hold on to the friendship when you find it, as it is rare.

Moreover, true friends are in each other's hearts and think about each other, even if you do not pick up the telephone to converse. That person is continually thought of in your heart of hearts and held constantly in prayer. You know without a shadow of a doubt, the same is reciprocated towards you.

You never lose the love for your friend just because you are not in each other's ears daily. As previously said, my true friends are dear to me, and it does not matter where they are or the distance between us. The bond has been made and cannot be easily broken.

True friends are forever. How about you? Are you a true friend to those you call friends? Are you being the best you to them? Do you make it all about you and not give them the opportunity to share their feelings? Are you friends just for what you can benefit from the other person?

CHAPTER VII
AS A GIRLFRIEND
(Once Upon A Time)

It has been a while, but I do remember the times when I was dating. There are so many memories, but I did not do much dating.

However, when I was about fifteen going on sixteen, I believe I was "in love". Cheesy, right? This guy was about 6' 4" tall, with light green eyes, very slender, but muscular built, and let us not talk about the smile, just breath taking.

During that time, I got butterflies thinking about him. I thought we were made for each other and the heavens were smiling on us (a true fifteen-year-old perspective).

I really liked this young man, and in my heart of hearts, I believed he liked me. He was about seventeen. I met his family and friends, and they were all great.

The relationship was long distance and he visited from time to time as he had relatives in my hometown. My friends and I also visited his country as well as the youth group from my church as our church associated with other Caribbean Churches. From a young girl perspective, I thought he was my knight in shining armor. Looking back, I often think, "what were you thinking?"

As a teenager, my thoughts were pure, and I really liked him until he said to me "let's have sex". I literally thought I was going to throw up. I felt so insulted, but being the best me to myself, I asked him "so after sex, what then?"

Of course, he could not answer. You know what happened next, the boyfriend/girlfriend ended. After that relationship was over, I didn't really date. I had secret crushes, but they remained secret.

When I was about seventeen, I dated, or I should say attempted to date, this guy who was tall, articulate, and very handsome. He was about twenty years of age. I do not know why I was attracted to older guys at that time.

He played the bass guitar, and his musical talent was undeniable. In addition, he treated me well and was very respectful. It was, however, short-lived, as he was older, and my parents were not consenting. I even got whipped just for speaking to him.

As you can tell, fortunately or unfortunately, growing up I did not have much of a boyfriend/girlfriend situation. In addition, I was not one that felt like I had to be dating throughout my teenage years.

I had goals and aspirations and I did not want anything or anyone to interfere with those attainable goals. Of course, I had guy friends, yes, just friends. The best me was saving myself for my husband.

There was this guy that I liked at one point, and we dated for literally two days. Why? I was in church, and I went outside for a minute (apparently, that is what young people did and still do, even today. You walk outside of church and people are standing outside for whatever reason). What do you think I saw while I was outside?

I witnessed him up close and personal with one of my good friends, confessing their love for each other; hilarious. Who would have thought? I am so proud of myself and how I handled the situation.

The best me very calmly told them, "wow, hope you are having fun and enjoying yourselves." After which, I went back inside. I would tell you his name, but it is so unique.

Those who knew me know who I am speaking about, and feathers might be ruffled. Although, it is good to sometimes ruffle feathers, the best me will not allow me to do so. Let's just say his name ended with "Sammy".

There you have it; I had a boring teenage dating life or lack thereof. However, the short-lived dating life that I had, the best me tried to always be kind and supportive; not much more I could have given from a teenager's perspective.

As I became a Christian at a young age, there was no crazy partying or anything of that nature. I was more focused on being a good girl and staying out of trouble. Also, let us not forget my dad, the fierce protector and no-nonsense father. I am proud that he was my dad.

He was indeed very strict, and I am glad he was that way. That is what a father does. Most guys were afraid to approach his daughters (six of us), and he put the fear in all of us and in them.

My Dad is now resting in the arms of Jesus, and I am grateful for the dad that he was. He loved his family very much, and we loved him. May he RIP.

Did I miss out on the crazy times that some of my friends indulged in? No, I did not. Some of those friends wish they had a do-over in life.

The best me appreciated the times and few dates I had, and those experiences contributed to who I am today. A woman of God, walking in faith and fulfilling my purpose.

I am happy to say this is me being the best me, as I am writing about my life. It is a wonderful life and I am truly blessed. If I could change anything, I would not change a thing.

If you are currently dating, take the time to know each other and do not be in a hurry to take your relationship to the next level. Take time to know yourself and what you desire in life.

Furthermore, do not let anyone force you into engaging in activities that you are not emotionally or mentally ready to participate in. Avoid succumbing to peer pressure. Just be you and do not try to be like anyone else.

Stand up for what you believe in and what you will tolerate. You drive the relationship and do not let anyone drive you. Also remember like the songwriter sings "you don't have to change a thing, the world can change its heart, you are beautiful, just the way you are" inside and out.

CHAPTER VIII
AS A SPOUSE

As I fast forward to the boyfriend, who is now my husband, I fell in true love at about 19 years of age, and what a lucky guy he is. After all these years, most of the time, I try to be the best me to him. Even those times when he is not deserving of me, I am still the best me.

It took some time to say yes to him being my boyfriend, but when I did, he was the happiest guy on earth. He won my priceless heart, and the best me makes him strive to be the best him.

He once said he feels lost without me, and you may wonder why. I have been told by friends and acquaintances that I am unforgettable, and that my personality draws people in. They like me even when they do not want to.

Keep reading and you may understand why I have that effect. It is possible that you too will gravitate towards me. I know you cannot believe I said that. Did I mention I had the gift of boldness?

Readers, you will understand why my "Boo" feels so lost without me. You have the proof that I am the best me to him, as the last time I checked, he is still among the living (just kidding). He is and will always be my "Boo".

The best me ensures his needs are met, and I mean all his needs. The ones he is aware of and even those he did not knew existed. Yes! There is only one me, and I am "the best me" to him and for him.

As a wife, I strive every day to please. It may be by breakfast in bed, calling to say I love you, or a million other ways. Should I count them? I cannot, as we do not have all that time and, we should not put a number on the amount of good we have done for others.

My boo is one of a kind, and I know it has taken a lot for him to stick around all these years. It is to his benefit, however, as each day (or should I say most days) he gets to experience part of the best me. I know your minds are wondering, but don't let it get the best of you.

With my husband, the best me comes naturally, especially if he is being his best self. I imagine he tries, as he knows a happy wife is a happy life and he likes happiness.

He does not always succeed, and there are countless scenarios I can mention. However, I will refrain from sharing the specifics. Just know that most of them were funny, and there were no repeats.

For the most part, he does try to listen and comprehend my needs which are not much. On rare occasions, he goes shopping at Victoria Secret. Nice, right? Having your spouse take the time to be so specific is endearing.

More importantly, it is impressive when they are successful in their choices as it can be hit or miss. Aiming to please the love of your life and pleasing that person is superb!

Our best selves produced and raised three beautiful, gifted, intelligent, and loving children. We thank God, each day for keeping them safe from the dangers of this ever-changing world.

How exciting it is to know that God however, does not change. I was blessed to obtain a scholarship to attend the University of Miami and received an EMBA (Executive Master of Business Administration) degree.

The best him (my spouse) supported the best me during this time. It gives me great joy to say thank you when someone shows me support. Therefore, I did not think twice to say thank you to him.

He was awarded with a special certification for his unending support through those hectic years of studies. That was me being the best me to him as he had given the best of himself to his family.

My husband made me proud and the best me acknowledged that I could not have completed my studies without his full support of being mom and dad to our children who were young at that time.

We had and still have our crazy times, but we always have each other's backs and currently have no intentions of quitting. It is through the tough and impossible times that we can either bring out the monsters or bring out the best selves.

We choose the latter or I should say, the best me chooses the latter. Also, the best me continues to pray for him in his weaknesses, and the best him uplifts me in my efforts to hold the family together. No one said it was or is going to be easy, but if we have each other, we will survive.

As a couple for several decades, we experience innumerable challenges daily; from a Christian perspective and from life in general. There were many times we wanted to quit on each other, but we remembered the good times outnumbered the bad and our best selves kept moving forward together.

Even as I write, we still have our moments when we feel like giving up but then our best selves think it through and pray about it. That is the reason why we are still together.

We are a family with grownups and are expecting our 1st grandson from our daughter, (the middle child). To us, our children will always be our little ones, and we will continue to do our best to inspire them and set the example for them to be their best selves.

Are you being your best selves to your family? Are you reflecting traits that your children can admire, or are you throwing in the towel? It is those times when you are challenged that you will see what you are made of. It is those times you will reflect who you really are.

I encourage you to be the best you and not succumb to the easiness of being who others may expect in tough situations. Remember people will always speak good and bad about you but never loose sight of who you are.

No one knows you better than you. Therefore, you have the power to enhance yourself and be the best you first for you and then for others. This will be a positive example for those around you.

For the most part, my life with my husband is great and it is a work in progress to become greater. We are the ones who determine what we would like our lives to be or not be. We do not have to mirror anyone or be like any one. It is in our DNA to be our best selves and pray that our lives will be meaningful to others.

The best me always chooses positivity over negativity. It takes so much energy to be negative. Why entertain that path when positivity is best? You decide if you prefer to be the best you to your family, and in doing so motivate your family and others to do the same.

CHAPTER IX
AS A MOTHER

Growing up, I always wondered what it would be like to be a mother, and I knew I wanted to be blessed with the experience. A year and a few months after marriage, I had the joy of becoming who I had longed to be, a mom.

It did not matter whether it was a girl or a boy. At one point my OBGYN mentioned there was a possibility of me having twins, as I had twin nephews, and my husband had twin siblings.

My first born was a boy, and his birth was one of the happiest days of my life. I looked at this little person with all his toes, fingers, eyes, nose, mouth, everything, and I was in heaven. He looked just like his dad, and we knew our lives would never be the same. We were embarking on a new family venture called parenting.

This little person depended on me for everything, and it was at that point that the best me fell in love with my mom all over again. I was compelled to call her and tell her how much I love her.

Having my son and seeing how much he relied on me to protect him, feed him, bathe him, wipe his runny nose, sing to him, make him smile, and simply care for him in every way was an experience I will never forget. I could be my best self continuously to this little person.

It was then I realized how much my mom had cared for my siblings and me without looking for anything in return. This was a new awakening, and I was in awe of the love you can feel for someone. This type of love is indescribable and unexplainable. It is simply true love.

My Mom loved us selflessly and helped us become the men and women we are today. Let us not forget the many sacrifices that were made on our behalf.

For all you daughters and sons, please cherish and love your moms. Let us not forget the dads. They also need our love and support.

They are irreplaceable, and you only have one of each. The caring I showed my first born is the same caring I did for the others as you will be privy to as you read on.

One day as I was picking up my four-year-old son from kindergarten, he started crying. I asked him what was wrong, and he told me "Rena" did not speak to him. I asked him who Rena was, and he told me it was his girlfriend whom he liked so much. She did not speak to him during the day, so he was very sad. Imagine a four-year-old feeling hurt by a little girl.

This left me speechless, and my first instinct was to yell, but the best me looked in his little face and beautiful eyes and said, "baby, don't cry. It is going to be okay. Rena must be having a bad day". I gave him hugs and kisses, and he quickly recovered.

He was exceptionally academically gifted and had the opportunity to attend private schools until his high school days. At the age of ten, he was rated in the top three percent of gifted students nationally, and at the age of eleven, he was recruited by Duke University to attend college.

This was a great feat. However, as parents we did not consent, as we did not feel he was emotionally ready for college life at such a young age. Yes, he was brilliant, but as a parent all factors need to be considered.

He continued to excel in school and graduated from Miami Dade College with a 4.0 GPA in Music Business. In the interim, as he tried to determine his next step, he pursued rap music and is a gifted lyricist.

The best me encourages him in his pursuit of happiness and supports his business endeavors to be the best him. He continues to have a positive outlook on life and is optimistic that his dreams will come to fruition.

There is no doubt that me continuing to be the best me to him will motivate him to continue to strive for greatness and be the best him. As mentioned, it did not matter what my first born was, I just wanted a healthy baby. With the second child, however, I wanted a daughter. I wanted a little me to dress-up. Little did I know my wish would come true.

My daughter came three weeks early and weighed 5lbs, 11 ounces. I was ecstatic and grateful for a healthy baby. She was gorgeous, and she was mine.

When I presented her to the world, my friends made their funny remarks, "where did you steal that gorgeous baby from?"

Interesting, since she looked like a combination of her dad and me. I really wanted to say, "don't hate, congratulate." I was over the moon. It is not my fault if you thought your babies were not equally gorgeous. I was and am happy with mine.

The best me held her tenderly and literally kept her close to my heart. She was my little princess, and I was going to protect her. Academically, she was another genius like her brother.

My daughter loved school. Rain or shine she wanted to attend. Her best self was very studios and she was the winner of the math competition within the Christian Private Schools in Florida and the salutatorian of her middle school.

In high school she graduated in the top 10 within a graduation class of over 200 students, who were all striving for excellence in their own rights.

Moreover, she was blessed and beyond words to be a recipient of the Presidential Scholarship to attend Florida International University, and she proudly accepted the honor.

Her course work in Arts and Science was very intense, but she persevered and succeeded in completing her studies. Subsequently, after graduating with a Bachelor of Science degree in Psychology, she took some well-deserved time off to regroup.

The best me did not pressure her to stay and further her studies, but I supported her decision to take off a year to explore what she wanted to do next, to prepare her for life at college. This was her securing her best self for the next chapter of her life.

Fast forward a year later, she pursued her graduate studies at Florida State University as an Art Therapist and graduated with a Master of Science Degree obtaining a 4.0 GPA.

The best me has always encouraged my children to be their best in every aspect of their lives. In addition, the best me always try to assist them in realizing their full potential.

As a gifted artist, my daughter brings out the best in her drawings; whether it is a drawing/painting of someone or something, she prides herself in her work reflecting the best of her in her craft.

While working as an Art Therapist, she challenges her students to express their feelings in their drawings, so she can better understand how to guide them. She offers her best self to them, so they can realize their best selves.

Being a mom is not easy, but it is a welcome challenge, and you can choose to be a great mom or an atrocious one.

Life is about choices, and I choose to be the best mom I possibly can.

As a result, I know I am truly loved, and I love them unconditionally. I have been blessed with a multi-talented/gifted daughter, who wears many hats in her career and personal life. She makes me proud.

By the time I have completed this book, I will be a grandma, and I intend to be the best me to my grandson. It is a blessing watching your children grow up into lovely men and women.

My daughter is ecstatic and cannot wait to be a mom. I told her he is going to give her a run for her money just like she did to me; all in good taste and fun.

She makes me proud and is my first in many things. First daughter, first child with a Master's degree, and first child to give me a grandchild. I have no worries, as the others are content with their life's journey.

You have read about my first two children, and they turned out great. You have one more to read about; my first exceptionally gifted musician, my third child and second son. It is ironic that I am writing about him today, April 27th (the day he was born.)

I discovered I was having a baby while I was visiting my relatives in the British Virgin Islands. It was kind of surreal as I had no idea I was pregnant.

One day while relaxing in bed with my husband and my other two children, I felt a movement in my stomach. Surely this could not be happening. I was in denial until I felt it again. Two days later I was back in Miami and at the gynecologist's office. He told me I was expecting my third child.

I was happy that I was having another baby boy, and I started to ponder how this one was very busy in my tummy, letting me know he was present.

For a moment, I thought I might be having twins as there was much activity happening on the inside. During my pregnancy, I made some changes with my gynecologist as we were not in sync.

I was blessed with a female gynecologist for the first time, and she was on point. She advised that I can expect my baby on April 27th. That is exactly what happened.

With the first two, my son came one week early, and my daughter came three weeks early. Third time around and blessed with a female gynecologist, she predicted the exact birth date. Just thought I would mention that little fact.

The best me, after having a C-Section, was a little overwhelmed from giving birth to a healthy 8lbs 11-ounce baby boy. I asked for a Big Mac and French fries immediately thereafter.

When I first saw him, I was overjoyed. My baby boy was big and healthy with so much hair and long lashes. I was delighted that all was well, and I knew this was the final chapter of giving birth.

Moving forward, I enrolled him in the private school with his sister, and at that school they offered music lessons. His sister was not interested in music, but he was. The instructor advised me after the 1st lesson that he is gifted.

Fast forward a few years, there were many competitions locally, statewide, and out of state. This involved much travelling and many investments. The best me always tried to support the goals and dreams of my children, and as I did with the others, so I did with him.

From winning Florida music competitions, gold medals in NAACP ACT-SO for music performance and composition, Young Artist Piano Showcase held in New York, and performing at Carnegie Hall, he was just getting started. Allow me to continue.

As a recording artist, lyricist, writer, sound engineer, music director, instructor, accomplished classical pianist, interim youth pastor, and holder of a Bachelor of Music Degree in Piano Performance from Florida State University, there is no doubt that we are blessed. Thank you, Lord, for Your many blessings!

This is the child that was very busy in the womb from a young age. I imagine he was playing the piano or one of the many instruments with which God has gifted him and preparing for what was and is to come.

One never knows, but one thing I know is that I am humbled and blessed to enjoy his talent. In addition, those who have had the privilege of meeting him voiced the same sentiments.

The best me continues to support and assist him with his musical career in booking/planning events, promoting his music; basically, working for him as his interim manager.

In addition, the best me reminds him to be humble (not that I need to) as he is most humble. I don't say that just because he is my son, but because I see the lifestyle he lives. It is a life of humility, and I am glad the best me sees the best him. I am glad to be his mother.

Your son or daughter may not be gifted in the ways my children are, but everyone has gifts with which they have been blessed. Therefore, encourage them to perfect their God-given gifts and be your best self to them.

All three of my children are a joy, and their lifestyles have influenced me to be the best me. We may not always agree with choices that our children make, but as parents we need to continuously encourage and support their dreams.

We cannot make them into us and have them live our dreams; they must live their own. Let us be our best selves to them so that they can be encouraged to be their best selves to their families.

The best me will never lose sight of their plight to become the young men and woman they are today; three wonderful, intelligent, and beautiful children, who I would not trade for anything or anyone.

They have brought me much joy, and the love we share is real. If I had to do it all over again, I would want to be blessed with these same children. They are the ones who keep me steadfast and energized to be the best me.

As mentioned, they are all now grown up and have their own lives, but as a family we will continue to be our best selves to each other. Along the way there were many mistakes, and growing pains.

However, those mistakes we made have framed who we are today, and we are thankful.

We do not know what tomorrow brings but we have each other and we can face life's greatest challenges together. I encourage you to hold on to your family and you will reap the promises you have made to each other.

How are you with your children? Are you being the best you to them? If not, it is never too late to start. And what better time than now? Be the best you, and you will have no regrets.

CHAPTER X
AS A PROFESSOR

While I was growing up, I had no intention of being a professor, but sometimes life takes you in different paths. You can choose to embrace or decline.

So how did I become an Adjunct Professor, you may ask? I ask myself the same question. It all happened while attending Trinity International University, where I did my undergraduate studies in Human Resources Management.

During my attendance at the university, I was enrolled in an accelerated program, and there were several presentations and research papers to be done. This is often challenging but I welcomed the opportunity to exceed the expectations.

The Director of the Administration was the professor for my research class. I was later told that she along with other professors were intrigued and impressed with my exceptional presentation skills, stage presence, and overall persona.

Subsequently, she (the director) was motivated to assist me in my career goals and recommended me to be a part of the University's faculty.

What do you do when opportunity comes knocking? You embrace the opportunity. I was grateful for the offer and humbly accepted the position of Adjunct Professor. I taught Business Ethics and Communication.

My first day at class rendered me nervous, and I sat in the classroom as a student waiting for the professor. This was kind of surreal as I had no idea I would ever be a professor.

When all the students were seated, they began inquiring and discussing the professor's whereabouts. It took everything in me to refrain from laughing. I ended the suspense at that time and introduced myself as the professor. The class was in awe as they thought I was a student and was too young to be a professor.

This was more than a decade ago. (Of course, they thought I was much younger than I was). The class was very diverse, which was a good thing. Diversity makes for good discussion.

I did the usual attendance call, an icebreaker to help them relax, and provided them with the course's syllabus/curriculum. This was a communication course. Therefore, speaking, listening, writing, and body language are all important factors. It was going to be fun.

As the classes continued, the students became comfortable and began to open and willingly participate in classroom discussions relative to the coursework. They also became very interactive with each other and ventured into other areas of discussions.

The best me motivated my students to realize their full potential and reminded them there are no goals that they cannot attain if they remained focused and persevered.

One student was a dancer with his own dance studio but wanted to major in Business. He felt that this would equip with the necessary tools to better manage the administrative aspects of his business.

However, he mentioned that he was not motivated until under my teachings. He saw my passion in helping and wanting them to succeed. This was the best me that he witnessed, and he was motivated to become his best self. It is every professor's dream to have inspired students.

Additionally, this said student advised he was relieved that the administration finally blessed them with a professor who understood their language and had the zeal to inspire them to achieve their goals.

As a professor, it was indeed a blessing to hear those words from one of my students; you feel fulfilled if you have at least helped one person to be his/her best self.

I am reminded of the scripture that says heaven rejoices whenever someone accepts Christ. When you have been a witness and you see the result of your work in another individual, it is a great feeling.

With this student being motivated, it was a domino effect, and before you knew it, the entire class was on the path to success. My coaching skills assisted them with putting forth their best work to earn the best grade one can attain, an A+. We know, however, that there is always at least one person who may try to create an upset. This class was no different and I was prepared.

The students were assigned a "term-paper" and to assist them, they were encouraged to provide me with a draft, so I can advise if they were on the correct path. This was standard protocol as it relates to term/research papers.

One of the students had a difficult time as she wrote the way she spoke, and unfortunately, there were many challenges. However, as promised, the best me made corrections and returned the paper.

As a professor, you can only do so much, or you find yourself doing the work for them. In college you need to think outside the box and be "a quick study," or you would be left behind.

I did encourage the students to return the paper to me as many times as needed to ensure they understood the directive and to meet me after class if they had questions or any concerns.

The student in question did not return the paper after the first corrections and she did not show interest in meeting with me. When a student does not take advantage of the opportunities presented, that student needs to be on top of his/her game.

Time went by, and the next time I saw her paper was when she submitted it to be graded. Most students received A's. This student received a B and was unhappy.

At the end of the class she expressed there were some concerns. I advised her to meet with me after class as I knew she was unhappy. When we met, she said she received a B and was upset because she knew one of the students did not attend one of the classes and received an A.

The best me explained to her that I will not be discussing her grade with any of the other students and therefore, I will not be discussing any of the other students grades with her.

I further informed her of the reasons why she received a B, which was very generous, considering that she did not take the time to review the corrections. Additionally, she did not accept the opportunity to meet with me for clarification on any of the corrections.

In addition, I discussed with her the areas where she needed improvement and encouraged her to enroll in specific writing courses to assist in her development.

She still was unhappy and reverted to speaking about other students' grades. The best me gently advised her that, as a student, it was her right to consult with the administration since she was unhappy.

I clearly communicated that I was not changing her grade since her work did not warrant such and reminded her I was very generous in the grade she received.

Yes, I know you may say that I was a little tough, but sometimes you need to enforce your standards and not be bullied into adhering to students' demands when the work is undeserving.

Readers, the best me will not mislead someone to believe their work is top notch when it is not. The best me must be truthful so that the students will understand the need to dedicate the time to accomplish their goals.

If the student wanted an A she needed to do the work. At the beginning of a semester, each student has an A. It is up to that student if he/she wants to maintain that A or allow it to decrease. Everyone decides to be their best self or settle for mediocrity.

Are you a student in college, hoping to bypass your studies and think you will still succeed in the end? Do you think you can intimidate your professor to change your grade to your liking?

Will you say it is fair for a professor to give you a good grade when your work is not reflective or deserving of such? How would you feel if your grade is compromised?

The student in question did engage the university's administration, and I am happy to say that my best self's decision earned the administration's reinforcing support. Be your best self, and the best you will prevail.

CHAPTER XI
AS A FASHIONISTA

Did I hear the word fashionista? That is my middle name. Although my name is uncommon, I do believe if you look up fashion you may find my name or see my picture.

Many people have various passions. I am proud to say I do too, and it is appearance. Yes, it has been this way from birth. I believe when I was born, I asked for a mirror, a pair of high heels, a designer dress, and a purse. Fashion is the very fiber of my being.

I am not sure why I am so passionate about the full wardrobe package, but I am, and it is too late to be eradicated from my system. I just love, love, love fashion.

For me, it does not necessarily need to be the latest trend or an expensive piece of clothing, but it must scream the wow factor when I look in the mirror. Simply saying it must be fashionable.

When I step out, I like to know that heads are turning even when they do not want to. Turning heads does not mean I am dressing to catch someone; I already did that. I have my husband.

However, it is a good feeling when you are admired, and people cannot help but take a second look. I know most of us can think of a scenario when we felt our best because we looked our best.

The best me does not and will not allow myself to be ordinary. Ordinary is not in my DNA. I must continuously stand in a positive and classy way. A way that most if not all will admire.

Did I hear you say confidence? Yes, I exude confidence, always have and always will. The best me strives to reflect the best characteristics and ensure self-confidence is at the top of my list. I do love myself and the more I love myself, I am better equipped to love others.

If you are a confident person, whatever you are selling, someone will purchase. Once you have someone's attention, you are already winning. Therefore, continue to be you, as I continue to be me and not worry what others are saying for they will continue to speak good and bad. It is human nature.

Let's talk about confidence, boldness, tenacity, and extroversion. These are all winning factors. Imagine if you are blessed with all of them, it is only a matter of time before you explode.

The best me at this moment is feeling mighty fine in owning up to all the above factors. Having these attributes are an asset to me writing this book. I feel blessed beyond measure.

To ensure there is no misunderstanding, it takes a certain type of person to write about their best self, and it takes a special audience to read and receive it. If you are reading this text, you are part of the audience. You are encouraged to invite your friends to participate and gain the understanding from my perspective of becoming a better you.

The audience that reads my book possesses a special desire in wanting to explore the angle I approach. You must be a very confident person to take time to read about me, a person speaking about my best self.

A co-worker once asked, "how do you do it? How do you always look your best while others look their worst even though they try?" It is my belief that the same dedication you put into any project should be put into yourself. If I am looking frumpy, I will behave the way I look.

Looking good makes me feel good and be good. I am a very happy person when I know I look good from head to toe. Please do not call me shallow. Some of you enjoy eating, decorating, gardening, exercising; I enjoy dressing. We all have different passions.

The best me chooses to look good, feel good, and be good. What is your passion? Does the best you make others feel good or make you feel good?

Remember, for me to be the best me to you, I must first be the best me to myself. Therefore, I first need to understand me for me to understand you. The same principle applies to you. You must first understand yourself before you can understand others.

Are you upset, or are you motivated to be the best you? In my junior year of college, I knew I wanted to always look good, therefore, I enrolled in in a self-development course.

It taught me how to expand my wardrobe to make it appear that I had many lines of clothing when that was not necessarily the case. In addition, this course taught me the fundamentals of having staple items in your closet and how to dress for success, among other things.

Furthermore, it motivated me to continue to be fashionable and to own my fashionista side. If you are identifying with something, do not be ashamed to own it. I know for me, it is a good feeling when I freely accept and embrace my beliefs.

When I was growing up, a guy said to me, "it does not matter what function you attend, the way you dress will always catch the eyes of everyone in the room". I am grateful that I can discern what looks best fashionably speaking.

Throughout the years, many have told me similar things such as "I do not know how you do it, but you always look impeccable and very classy". Others have said I have an undeniable presence I light up the room. These are all encouraging words, and I am humbled.

As we age, we sometimes think that we are no longer beautiful, classy, or sexy. Do not believe those lies. For me, Venoria Todman, I have been, I am, and will continually be classy, sexy, and beautiful. Do I need to repeat myself?

The best me currently is and will always be classy, sexy and beautiful. I do not let my age define me, I define my age. The best me is advising you, to do the same. You are the one in control, not your friends or acquaintances. You map out the way you would like things to go, now watch and give thanks.

Additionally, do not let your clothes wear you; you wear your clothes. Being sexy does not mean wearing tight, skimpy, or revealing clothing. You can be all covered up and be as sexy as you want to be. Just remember these clothes were made for wearing, so wear them well.

We are sometimes confused with sexy and classy. Please keep in mind they are not the same but can go well together. For example, gracefulness, boldness, and confidence, can be considered both classy and sexy and you should wear them well. Do not be afraid to embrace what you were blessed with. God gave it to you so be thankful and unashamed to use it for good.

Furthermore, please do not believe everything you are told. Use a mirror as much as you can for validity. However, at times a mirror may reflect deceit, therefore, seek the advice of a true friend who is going to be honest with you. Do not be upset when you are told the truth. Receive it and make the necessary adjustments.

If your friend tells you a specific outfit is not working, you may want to pay attention. If you are a size eight and trying to fit in a size four, that probably will not work properly. You may need the "fashion police".

As a fashionista, the best me is advising you that just because it is trending does not mean it compliments you. It is the same with hairstyles. Not all hairstyles are for everyone.

For the most part, I do my best to keep it together, but every now and then, the best fashionistas, including me, have little mishaps. Consequently, when things do not go as planned, make sure the next time you step out, you are "slaying".

The best me is open for constructive criticism. Therefore, I sometimes seek the advice from my mini me, and she lets me have it. Even my husband, at times, will let me know, "this one is not working for you".

Truth be told, as a fashionista, I know when it is not working, and those are the few times I would ask for a second opinion. When it is working, I do not need clarification. I just step out and work it. Those are the times when my confidence is to the moon.

I remember in the early 2000's, I won a raffle and it involved a wardrobe expert from a "Dressing for Success", Company to come to your home, go through your wardrobe, make suggestions, and take you shopping. Some of my co-workers voiced, "ironically, of all the people who could have won, you did".

The business mogul came to my home, when all kids still lived at home, so I was in a much larger home with a considerably large closet. It was also well organized, and everything was in its proper place.

When she went through my wardrobe she said I made her job easy as there were no tips to give. She mentioned she was impressed and that I had it down pact. I was happy to hear those comments.

We did go shopping, and we were able to purchase three different outfits from the funds they allotted to her to expand my wardrobe. It was so exciting to be shopping with an actual wardrobe genius.

I am also reminded of the time I met my late mother-in-law for the first time. She said to me, "I have heard a lot about you, especially about the way you carry yourself. They told me the girl my son is dating is a movie star, and now I know why".

Since I was a child, I have always believed in looking my best and as I became older, that belief transcended into dressing for success. I am proud to know people took notice then, as obviously they talked about it. Therefore, I must have made a positive impression then, and subsequently, still making positive impressions.

As a fashionista, the best me ensures my better half, my husband, is looking fabulous as well! I cannot be stepping out looking like my best self, and the better part of me is down a notch. We complement each other as we strive to be in sync. Be the best you to your boo.

CHAPTER XII
THE BEST ME TODAY

Writing this book has been an awesome journey. There has been so much fun and laughter as I discovered and remembered things about myself. I did not realize that writing about the best me will also help me to be the best me or a better me.

The best me as a friend, sibling, wife, mother, Christian, student, professor, and fashionista, are all so surreal. I am inspired to always try to be the best me while encouraging others to do the same and be their best selves.

Today, the best me is determined to keep reaching towards higher goals, being my best self not only to family and friends, but to all those I encounter. Please remember kind words to a stranger may uplift him/her and may save a life.

We go about our lives each day not knowing what others are going through and sometimes fail to demonstrate love and compassion. We need to take some time to think about others and show that we care.

A simple hello to someone may prevent that person from inflicting harm. A simple smile, may uplift someone's spirit. How about a hug, or just saying good morning?

Think about it, we put on our nice clothes, drive in our fancy cars to our nice high-paying jobs and go home to our warm beds. The reality, however, is people are hurting. Somewhere in a dark lonely place, people are hungry, kids are crying, and parents do not know how they are going to feed their children.

Therefore, the best me in me encourages me and all of us to think of the homeless, the hungry, the weary, and the forgotten among us. Think on those who are broken in spirit and need someone to assure them it is going to be okay.

They all have needs, and those of us who are truly blessed beyond measure, not only need to pray but to act upon it and let our best selves help those who are less fortunate. Keep in mind to always ask yourself the question, "what would Jesus do?"

The best me today is not the best me yesterday. Each day I strive to be a better me. Better me as a friend, Christian, wife, mother, and yes, even a fashionista. Remember, when I look good I feel good. When I do good I am good.

How are you today compared to yesterday? Are you your best self or are you pretending to be? Do you enjoy being your best self to your family and friends? What about strangers, do you shrug your shoulders and pretend that they do not exist, or do you aspire to help them?

Are you ashamed to acknowledge Christ? And, are you walking in newness of life? Let us always strive to assist those that are less fortunate.

Remember, I mentioned earlier that by the time I am finished writing this book, I will be a Grandma? Well I am. My daughter and her husband of four years, welcomed their beautiful son, Kendrick, on May 31st, 2017.

My life is now more enriched as I FaceTime with him and see the joy he has brought to all of us. He is such a blessing and I am the proud Grandma. He smiles and speaks in a language that we think we understand. Just a glimpse of him will melt your heart and to know him is to love him.

Kendrick, when you grow up and have an opportunity to read this book, "The Best Me" my prayer for you is to always be your best self and demonstrate the love that Christ has for us and has taught us. My precious grandson, you are a beautiful person and you are unique. There is no one like you and there is nothing you cannot do. You are destined for great things and you will be successful. When you are blessed be sure to bless others. Love you, love you, love you!

The best me today is a loyal friend, awesome sibling, loving mother, devoted wife, glamorous grandma, Spirit-filled Christian and yes, I am still sexy, classy and beautiful.

Yesterday, today and forever, I will always strive to be the best me. Here I am today, an Author and CEO/Founder of my publishing company, Mystique Journal, established in 2015. "The Best Me"; that is my brand and title of my second book.

I am confident that this book "The Best Me" is slated to capture existing and new readers. It is my belief that everyone desires to reflect the best of themselves. All they need is encouragement along the way and belief that they are good enough to do anything and accomplish their goals.

How about you? Will you strive to be the best you? Will you settle for being what others want you to be? What is your brand? Everyone has a brand, whether it is intentional or unintentional.

Let your brand be something that makes you proud. Therefore, strive to be your best self even when no one is looking or seems to be looking. Search your heart and be reminded that each of us has a best self that is waiting to exhale.

CHAPTER XIII
CONCLUSION

Readers, once again we have traveled together. This time on a different journey. You have seen me as the best me encouraging you to be the best you. I am sure you were inspired and at times, you probably wanted to yell.

Some of you may feel I am self-centered, and others may feel I am uplifting. Whatever your feelings, I am glad you have traveled on this journey with me. There is so much more to be said and much more to explore.

I encourage you to love yourself and always be reminded you are worth the effort. Every time you look in the mirror, every time you are awake, know that you are unique, and there is no one like you. You are beautiful and wonderfully made.

You have the power to determine your behavior. No one knows you like you, just like no one knows me like me.

We have strengths and, of course, weaknesses. There is good and bad in all of us. Some of us more good than bad and some, unfortunately, more bad than good.

For the latter, do not feel you are less worth it. Christ did not cherry-pick who he died and resurrected for, as all of us have sinned and fall short of God's glory, but when he hung on the cross, he bore all our shame and guilt.

Who is to say your sin is worse than mine or mine is lesser than yours? In God's eyes, it is all sin. However, if we confess our sins, he is faithful and just to forgive us and cleanse us from all unrighteousness.

Therefore, let us not be weary in trying to be our best selves. The more we try, the better we will become. Being the best you and me being the best me is like an athlete. Each play, each practice, he learns to perfect his craft.

With us, the more we do good and be our best selves, it becomes natural, and soon we will not have to exert a special effort. You will be the best you and I will the best me.

The best me still has struggles and challenges but they do not deter me from greatness, which is part of the best me in me. I like saying those words, I like writing them.

Each time I write the words the best me, I am empowered to be the best me and give of my best self. It can be challenging at times, but the result is rewarding.

You will have good and bad days. Enjoy the good ones and do not give in to the bad and lose a part of your best self. Find the courage to turn them into better ones. Furthermore, rise above them and find new strength to renew your best self and be the best you.

There are people depending on you and looking to you for guidance. They have seen the best and the worst of you and they still love you. Therefore, I admonish you to love you too.

When you give of your best self, you feel good, don't you? I know I do. Therefore, I will continue to be the best me and give of my best self every time the opportunity presents itself and when no opportunity seems to be present, the best me will create ways and opportunities to reflect my best self.

Yes, it is difficult to always be your best self, but each of us has the ability. Therefore, let us not stop striving for greatness, for new heights, and new depths. We can achieve whatever we desire by giving 100% of our best selves.

Be inspired and know that there is nothing you cannot achieve if you are focused and not distracted with pettiness. Take the time to set your goals and aspirations and do not let anyone stand in your way of attaining success.

Let us persevere and internalize the best in us and then externalize, so the world would see and know that "yes, we can, yes, we will, and yes, we did". The best me, the best you, the best us!

Thank you for reading

V.T. Author

www.ingramcontent.com/pod-product-compliance
Lightning Source LLC
LaVergne TN
LVHW041627070426
835507LV00008B/498